AF072615

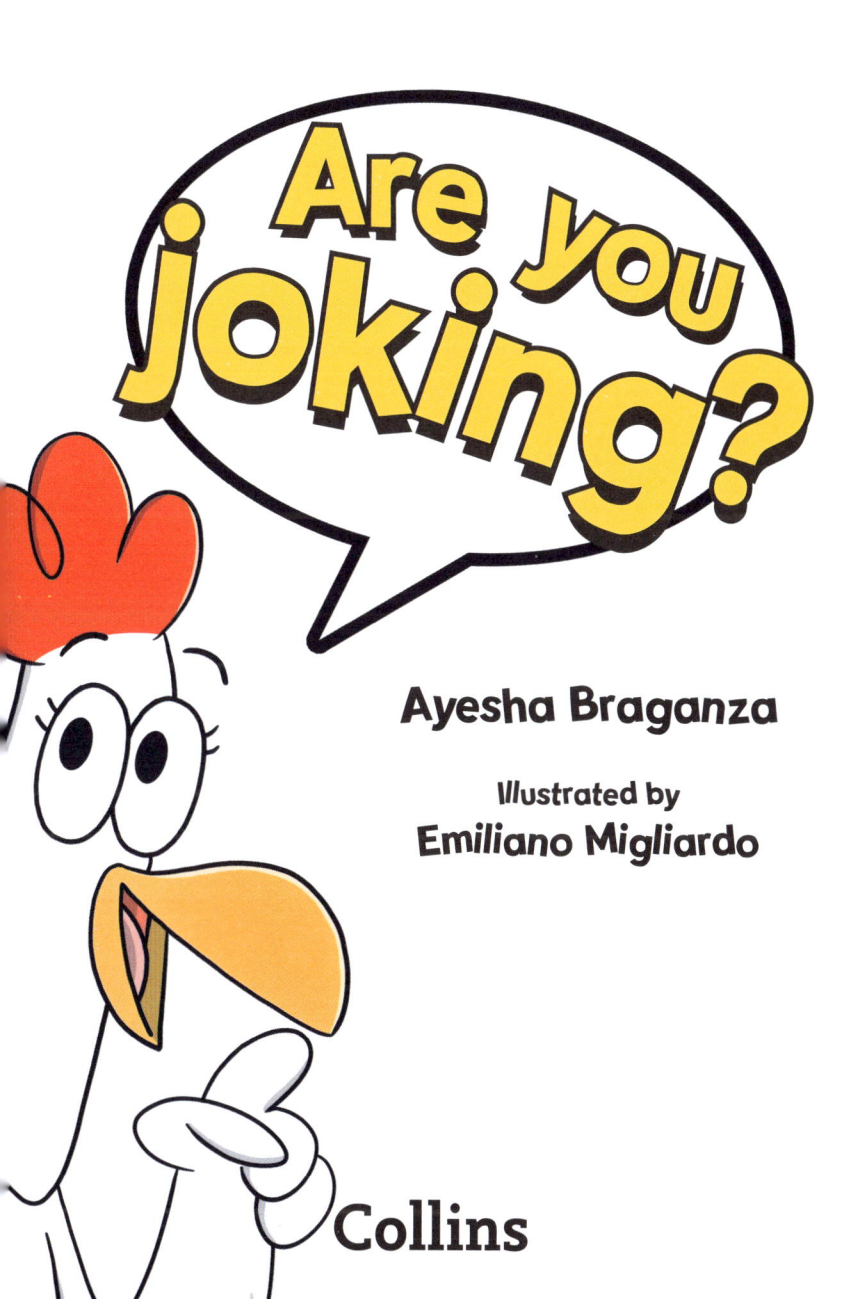

Are you joking?

Ayesha Braganza

**Illustrated by
Emiliano Migliardo**

Collins

Contents

Chapter 1 What is a joke? 6

BONUS Joke library 20

Chapter 2 Jokes, ancient and modern 22

BONUS Joke timeline 36

Chapter 3 Popular jokes 38

BONUS Match the setup to the punchline 52

Chapter 4 Physical comedy 54

BONUS Make up your own funny sketch 70

Chapter 5 Having fun around the world 72

BONUS Festival map 88

Chapter 6 What happens when we laugh? .. 90

BONUS Feel-good chemicals 104

About the author 106

About the illustrator 108

Book chat 110

Chapter 1
What is a joke?

A joke is something that makes people laugh. Some jokes can be spoken.

> Why did the banana go to the doctor? Because he wasn't peeling well.

> I love funny word mix-ups like 'feeling and peeling'. Ha!

Some jokes are written.

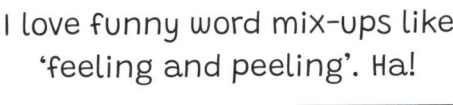

> Why did the chicken cross the road?

> Because she thought it was an EGG-cellent idea!

> Great! I just LOVE crossing roads!

Other jokes are practical, involving physical actions such as funny pranks or tricks. For example, we might think it's funny to see someone getting a custard pie thrown in their face. Although this is the interesting thing about jokes – not everyone finds custard pie throwing funny. So, we can see that what makes a joke funny varies between different people.

Jokes can also be told in pictures.

They can even be told through music. For example, sometimes a piece of music is interrupted by a comedy 'honking' noise that makes listeners laugh.

What makes a joke?

Jokes are often told in similar ways. For example, many jokes involve a:

Setup – like a question or something we expect to happen

and a

Punchline – which is the funny answer to the question or situation. This might poke fun at someone or something, change what we expect to happen, or play with words that sound the same.

> Where do fish keep their money?

> In the river bank.

This punchline relies on wordplay, as a river bank means the muddy land on the side of a river, but 'bank' also means a place where we keep our money.

How to tell a joke

Now we know what makes a joke, let's learn how to tell a joke and make it funny.

1. Choose the right joke for your audience.

> Where do you find a dog without any legs?

> Exactly where you left them!

This might not be the best joke to tell someone who loves dogs!

2. Know your joke well.

You will have to memorise your joke – that is, learn it by heart. This is so you don't stumble over the punchline, which will spoil your joke.

3. Timing

It is all about timing.

Don't rush the setup: the slower you tell your joke, the more likely your audience will understand it. Pause briefly before your punchline, as this creates suspense and makes sure people are following you. You can use your voice and how you move your body to help you. Try practising with this joke.

Setup – Why don't skeletons go to parties? (Maybe use your face and voice to show you are asking a question. Pause for a few seconds to let your audience think.)

Punchline – Because they have no *body* to go with! (Perhaps emphasise the word 'body' so that your audience gets the wordplay of your joke – that the skeleton has no body because it's made of bones, and that the skeleton has no one – 'nobody' – to go to the party with.)

Why jokes work

Jokes work because they often have certain elements in common that make them funny. For example:

1. Relatability

Some jokes work because they are about an experience that we all share.

> How do you know the ocean is friendly?

It waves!

This joke is relatable because most people know about ocean waves and hand waves too.

2. Exaggeration

Jokes can be based on exaggeration that makes the punchline ridiculous and unexpected because it's so over-the-top.

> Mum, Mum, there is a dog outside and it's the size of an elephant.

> Son, I have told you 500,000 times not to exaggerate!

3. Wordplay

We've already read a few of these types of jokes. They use puns, which are jokes that rely on similar sounding words (like fun and run) or words with the same sound but different meanings (like sea and see).

> What animal always cheats on tests?

> A cheetah!

Types of jokes

One-liners
These are one-line setups with one-line punchlines.

> What is a witch's favourite subject?

> Spell-ings!

See if you can find any other examples of one-liners in this book.

Knock-knock, doctor doctor and chicken jokes
These are classic jokes that usually start in the same way.

> Why is the chicken so funny?

> She's a real comedi-hen!

> Egg-cellent! A chicken joke!

> As with all the best jokes, this is wordplay. A comedian tells jokes for a living and sounds similar to 'comedi-hen'!

Riddles

These are questions that make us very curious, as the answer seems impossible.

What comes once in a minute, twice in a moment, but never in a thousand years?

The letter 'M'!

What is full of holes but still holds water?

A sponge!

Do you think that riddles are actually jokes? Look back at the definition of a joke at the start of this chapter. Do riddles make you laugh?

Dark humour

Sometimes people use humour to laugh at difficult subjects like death, illness or bodily functions. This might make them feel less scared or disgusted.

Why are graveyards always popular?

Because people are dying to get in!

Self-deprecating jokes

Self-deprecating jokes are jokes that people tell to make themselves or their abilities seem less important. People may tell jokes like this as a way of stopping others from making jokes about them, or to get others to like them.

I love my running exercise routine. It includes running away from problems and running late!

Sarcasm and irony

An ironic joke comes from saying the opposite of what is really meant.

Sarcastic jokes often poke fun at other people or situations.

Limericks
Limericks are funny five-line rhyming poems.

There once was a farmer from Leeds

Who swallowed a packet of seeds.

It soon came to pass,

He was covered with grass,

But has all the tomatoes he needs.

Joke library

What time do you go to the dentist?

Tooth-hurty.

What did the policeman say to his tummy?

You're under a vest!

What's brown and sticky?

A stick!

I'd tell you the joke about the butter but you'd spread it!

Knock knock.

Who's there?

Boo boo.

Boo boo who?

It's ok, no need to cry.

Why did the dinosaur cross the road?

Because chickens didn't exist yet.

Why do you put bulbs in the ground?

So the worms can see.

Why did the children eat their homework?

Because their teacher told them it was a piece of cake!

Chapter 2
Jokes, ancient and modern

The oldest joke (1900 BCE)

It's impossible to know what the first joke was, as nobody wrote it down.

Maybe one cave man or woman laughed at another when they tripped over, or perhaps they hid the cooking pot and giggled as they watched the other person looking for it.

What *is* clear is that the world's oldest known recorded joke comes from Sumer (modern-day southern Iraq) and dates as far back as 1900 BCE. It's a bit rude and involves a person farting!

Ancient Egyptian jokes

Ancient Egyptian art often portrayed animals in human roles. This was visual humour that was funny because people didn't expect to see animals acting like humans.

For example, the Satirical Papyrus of Turin (1150 BCE) is a famous example of Egyptian humour. It shows animals taking on human roles in absurd situations. The image below is from the papyrus and shows a lion and an antelope playing a board game.

Ancient Greek comedy

Plato was an ancient Greek philosopher. He was so against humour that he banned it from his school, the Academy. That's no joke! He was represented by comedians in Athens as a 'grouch' – someone with no sense of humour.

Comedy as a form of entertainment started in Athens and comes from the Greek word *komos* meaning a noisy, happy procession of people.

Ancient Roman jokes

The ancient Roman playwright Plautus wrote his plays about 2,200 years ago. He liked using physical humour and slapstick, and his plays often took a topsy-turvy view of life. In Plautus's plays, servants gave orders to their masters, and children outwitted their parents.

The ancient Romans also enjoyed practical jokes. One of the oldest practical jokes involved a 14-year-old Roman emperor, Heliogabalus. He played a joke on his dinner guests that involved them sitting on deflating cushions that 'farted'.

Ancient Indian humour

Humour in ancient India can be found in folktales, plays and sacred texts. Like other ancient cultures, it uses wordplay and exaggeration to make fun of human behaviour.

The Panchatantra is a collection of animal stories that teach wisdom through funny dialogue. Here is a summary of one story:

A nasty lion keeps eating the other jungle animals. A clever hare tricks the lion by pretending another lion is trying to take over his territory.

The hare shows the lion his reflection in a deep well. The lion thinks his reflection is the other lion, so he jumps in to attack it — and drowns!

Jokes in the Middle Ages

In the Middle Ages, some people actually had the job of telling jokes and entertaining others through humour. Some of them became famous, like Nasreddin Hodja in the Middle East, who was well known for his clever jokes.

A Nasreddin joke goes:

The first printed joke

The invention of the printing press allowed jokes to be distributed to more people. Around 550 years ago, the first joke book was printed: *Facetiae*, by Poggio Bracciolini. This was a collection of funny stories and jokes.

A poor man was caught stealing bread from a bakery. When the baker asked him why he was stealing, he said:

"I wasn't stealing. I was borrowing the bread!"

Stand-up comedy

In the 19th and early 20th centuries, music halls in the United States and Britain popularised vaudeville. Vaudeville is a theatrical type of comedy that can include comedy sketches, magic, musical acts, acrobatics and physical comedy. Stand-up comedians performed jokes in theatres for a living. Performers like Groucho Marx delivered rapid-fire one-liners, like this one:

> This is such a simple job a four-year-old child could understand what to do.
>
> Quick, get me a four-year-old child to help me – I don't understand what to do!

pairs

Chocolate disaster

From around 70 years ago, television brought humour into people's homes. *I Love Lucy* (1951–1957) was one of the first 'sitcoms' – situational comedies – on TV. These sitcoms had short episodes based around regular characters in ordinary situations.

Lucy dreamed of being a star, but always got into trouble. The jokes were very physical, like her famous Chocolate Factory scene where she is employed to wrap chocolates that appear on a conveyor belt. As the machine speeds up, Lucy tries to keep up by stuffing chocolates in her mouth and hiding them under her hat and shirt!

Rubber chickens

Milton Berle, the American comedian, brought the vaudeville style to TV. He used a lot of physical comedy, like exploding microphones, collapsing chairs, and glasses that would unexpectedly spray water over his guests. He was also famous for randomly throwing a rubber chicken around the stage. A Milton joke:

My neighbour told me he had a pet chicken. I told him 'That's an EGG-citing pet!'

I love Milton Berle. He was the first to make chickens funny. I'm not a fan of throwing them, though.

Internet humour

Today, the internet has changed the way we tell jokes. We now have memes – humorous images and text we share online – videos and cartoons. Online humour is faster, more interactive and ever-changing.

Online humour works in the same way as other forms of jokes. Simple ideas for memes work because they are relatable. Or they rely on exaggeration.

The internet has also popularised other forms of jokes, like funny fails in games like Minecraft. Some viral videos involve changing the voices of well-known people to make them sound ridiculous or adding over-the-top sound effects like BOING!

Wordplay and silly sentences can become viral jokes, such as 'What if milk was called cow juice?' Intentional misspellings and funny phrases have become huge parts of humour on the internet.

Joke timeline

BONUS

1900 BCE
First recorded joke – about farting!

1150 BCE
The Satirical Papyrus of Turin

Today
Internet humour and memes go viral

1950s
First TV sitcom airs

175 BCE
Plautus' plays and Roman fart cushion

mid-1400s
First joke book printed

1800s–1900s
Stand-up comedy is popularised

Chapter 3
Popular jokes

Sometimes a particular type of joke suddenly becomes really popular. This happened with knock-knock, chicken and doctor-doctor jokes.

Who knocked first?

No one is certain who invented the first 'knock-knock' joke. Some people think it was the English playwright William Shakespeare. His play *Macbeth* was first performed in 1606, and one of the characters repeatedly says, 'Knock-knock! Who's there?' The answer is to do with a murder – so the first knock-knock joke was far from being a harmless bit of fun!

In the past, there was a craze for knock-knock jokes like this one.

Here is one example:

Joking like this used to be considered a sickness by some people! It's true! In the 1930s, knock-knock jokes were everywhere. Businesses staged knock-knock contests, orchestras wove them into their music and they were used in adverts. For example, in the United States, The Edgmont Cash and Carry grocery store ran this display advert in a newspaper:

> Knock knock.
>
> Who's there?
>
> Don.
>
> Don who?
>
> Don forget to do your shopping at the Cash and Carry ....

However, some said 'no, no' to knock knock as they were worried that people were getting addicted to this form of joke telling.

The first chicken joke

The first known version of the famous chicken joke (you know the one – 'Why did the chicken cross the road?') appeared in 1847 in *The Knickerbocker*, a New York magazine.

The Knickerbocker was a monthly magazine that was about more than just jokes. It also included fiction, true stories and eye-witness accounts of real-life events that were hitting the news at the time.

The first ever chicken joke went like this:

> Why did the chicken cross the road?

> Because it wanted to get to the other side!

It is an unusual joke, because you might expect a clever punchline to answer the question. Instead, the answer is very straightforward. This 'anti-joke' style made the ordinary answer funny.

> Wow, this is the first time I got to cross a road. How many roads do you think I've crossed since 1847? A lot!

Why are chickens funny?

People have told animal jokes for a long time – often telling them out loud rather than writing them down. Chickens are common farm animals and in many communities they are part of everyday life. They're easy to picture, and their movements are quite jerky and naturally funny, so it's not surprising they became the basis of jokes.

The chicken joke became part of children's joke collections in the 19th and early 20th century. Here's an example from a 1920s joke book:

Why did the chicken cross the playground?

To get to the other slide!

You know, that's not just a chicken joke, it's wordplay too.

Chicken jokes and social media

The internet has given the classic chicken joke a new lease of life. Social media and meme culture thrive on remixing classic jokes. For example:

Why did the chicken cross the road?

To avoid this joke!

Platforms like YouTube and TikTok have popularised short videos, some of which are based on chicken jokes. The videos expand the joke visually, for example, turning the chicken's journey crossing the road into an epic Hollywood film-type quest.

One example that went viral was accompanied by a dramatic movie trailer voiceover:

One chicken.
One road.
One destiny.

Visiting the doctor can be a joke

One of the earliest joke books dates from around one thousand years ago! It's called *Philogelos*, meaning 'laughter-lover', and it includes 265 jokes. *Philogelos* contains some early doctor-doctor jokes, like this one:

Doctor, when I wake up, I'm dizzy for half an hour before I start to feel better.

Wake up half an hour later then!

Doctor-doctor jokes often rely on wordplay and absurdity. For example:

This relies on the double meaning of 'ring' – the sound of a bell, or a phone call.

Can you spot the double meaning in this example?

Patient: Doctor, doctor, I've got wind! Can you give me something for it?

Doctor: Yes, here's a kite!

Wizard wordplay

Many jokes feature wordplay (also known as puns). Wordplay relies on having fun with words that have multiple meanings or similar sounds to create the joke. In fact, the word 'joke' comes from the Latin word *jocus* meaning 'wordplay'.

A pun relies on different meanings for the same word. For example:

Why don't elephants use computers?

Because they're afraid of the mouse!

This uses the two different meanings of the word 'mouse' to create the joke.

Wordplay is my favourite kind of magic.

Wordplay can make use of different meanings in clever ways:

People all around the world and across many different languages enjoy wordplay and pun humour. This Japanese pun relies on wordplay about the word *mikata*, which means both friend and tangerine.

> *Nande mikata wa shiawase na no?* –
> Why are tangerines happy?

> *Mikan wa minna no mikata da y!* –
> Tangerines are everyone's friends!

Pokémon characters use Japanese wordplay in their names. For example, Charmander's Japanese name is 'Hitokage', with 'hito' meaning 'fire' and 'kage' meaning 'lizard' – so 'fire lizard' describes Charmander's fiery tail and reptile-like appearance.

In West African cultures, wordplay sometimes relies on different ways of pronouncing the same words.

For example, in Yoruba, there is a joke:

> Let's eat pounded yam, not troubles!

In Yoruba, this is:

> E je ka je iyan ma je ka kan.

Iyan means 'pounded yam', but it can also sound like the word 'troubles' in Yoruba (kan). So, this is a humorous way of encouraging people to enjoy eating together and avoid life's troubles.

BONUS

Match the setup to the punchline

What do lions eat?

Why can't you trust stairs?

What happens when two giraffes collide together?

Where do cows go on a Friday night?

How do you throw a space party?

Why do giraffes have long necks?

The moooooovies.

You planet.

Because their feet smell.

Because they're always up to something!

Roarrr meat!

A giraffic jam.

Chapter 4
Physical comedy

Physical comedy is a type of humour based on body movements, facial expressions and physical actions, rather than relying on words.

It's likely that physical humour is as old as the human race! It's easy to imagine that long before language developed, our ancestors entertained themselves with funny physical tricks and body language. And once people had words to express themselves with, they still found physical humour funny.

Physical comedy was popular in ancient times. The Roman playwright Plautus wrote a play called *Miles Gloriosus*, which means 'The Swaggering Soldier'. In this play, servants try to fool their master in a comedic way that involves pretend falls and silly chases.

Who is the real fool?

In medieval times, physical comedy gained even more popularity, with 'jesters' doing street performances involving juggling and acrobatics. They were as colourful as modern-day clowns, often wearing unusual clothes in contrasting bright colours, and pointed hats with bells on the end.

Jesters were not only street entertainers but were also found in medieval royal courts, where they entertained kings and queens. They could make lots of money if they kept the royal family amused.

But life wasn't always easy for jesters. If a joke didn't work, or if the jester accidentally insulted someone important, they could easily be sacked. And they often had to travel with the royal court to battles, where they were expected to entertain the soldiers and even join in with the fighting!

Jesters were mostly male, but there were a few famous female jesters. One was Mathurine, who was a jester to French kings in medieval times. She had fantastic costumes and dressed up as lots of different characters, including a warrior, complete with a wooden sword.

A joke we have from Mathurine:

From medieval to modern

Around 500 years ago, jester-like characters like Pierrot and Harlequin, shown below, began to be popular. Both of these influenced modern-day clowning.

Harlequin   Pierrot

Joseph Grimaldi, from England, is considered the father of modern clowning, with his makeup, elaborate costumes and use of physical slapstick comedy. Grimaldi lived about 200 years ago. When he was in his twenties, he gained his greatest success in a pantomime called *Harlequin Mother Goose*. For this show, he created a new kind of cheeky clown character that used slapstick and influenced lots of other clowns and pantomime performers.

Slapstick at last

Slapstick is a type of physical comedy. The humour relies on make-believe fights and exaggerated physical movements. Originally, the 'slapstick' itself was two wooden sticks that would smack together, creating a loud slapping noise. So, one actor could pretend to hit another really hard but without harming anyone.

The word 'punchline' comes from Punchinello, who was a mean slapstick puppet. Later, Punchinello developed into the puppets we know today as Punch and Judy, whose slapstick humour still draws big laughs. Slapstick comedy is also a major part of clowning.

Dangerous clowning

Clowning is found all over the world. In the United States and Canada, over 120 years ago, clowns used to take part in bull-riding competitions. It was very dangerous, because the clown had to protect the bull-riding cowboy when he fell off the bull. The clown did this by distracting the bull so that it would run towards the clown. This would stop the bull from trampling the fallen rider, and allow him time to escape. These rodeo clowns would wear bright clothing and makeup. They would use noisy, colourful props to distract the bull – like inflatable chickens and exploding garbage cans.

A famous Russian clown

Oleg Popov was a famous Russian clown who had a unique look with a chequered hat. He started learning his circus skills as a teenager and combined magic, tightrope walking and juggling to make people laugh. He became so famous, he won many awards in Russia, including The People's Artist award in 1969. One of his acts involved balancing a real chicken on a pole.

Physical humour was also very present in early 'silent' films, over 100 years ago. These films were silent because the technology to include sound hadn't been developed yet. Charlie Chaplin was an early silent film actor, creating many famous characters, including the Tramp. The Tramp dressed in baggy trousers, a tight coat, a bowler hat, oversized shoes and had a cane. He got involved in a lot of funny, physical comedy.

In one film, he tried to eat an egg complete with its shell! Yuck!

Buster Keaton was another important silent film performer who started out in films about 100 years ago. He was famous for his physical comedy, combining impressive stunts and slapstick with a very serious, deadpan facial expression.

The popularity of physical humour continues today, with characters like Mr Bean. Mr Bean doesn't talk, but he makes funny faces and silly sounds. The humour is visual – like when Mr Bean gets a stone in his shoe and takes it off to investigate. Unfortunately, he puts his shoe and sock on top of a car which drives off, leaving him hopping about!

Mr Bean: that's classic slapstick humour, you know!

Exaggerated slapstick continues in cartoon form. In SpongeBob SquarePants, SpongeBob has a rubbery body. In one sketch, he slips on a banana peel and turns into a tangled pretzel before snapping back to normal.

Platforms like YouTube and TikTok have changed how physical comedy is performed and edited. Digital effects can create 'magic tricks' that enhance physical comedy stunts, like jumping into a painting, walking through a mirror or turning a drawing of a pizza into the real thing.

Many YouTubers use fast-paced, edited physical comedy and extreme physical challenges and mishaps. For example, they popularise challenges involving giant food fights, slime dumps or water balloon wars.

Make up your own funny sketch

BONUS

Choose one or two characters (funny characters don't have to be human).

Choose a location (does the action take place at school, home, the playground, a pool?).

Chapter 5
Having fun around the world

What people find enjoyable and funny can vary widely around the world, and what one person in one country finds fun or funny, another may not. It's important to respect the difference between cultures, backgrounds and senses of fun and humour.

In this chapter, there are examples of traditions from around the world that bring enjoyment to those who participate, and they also show that the ways we celebrate and have fun are different across the world.

You'll see that a lot of the events featured in this chapter have one thing in common – they involve physical humour and funny situations rather than relying on words!

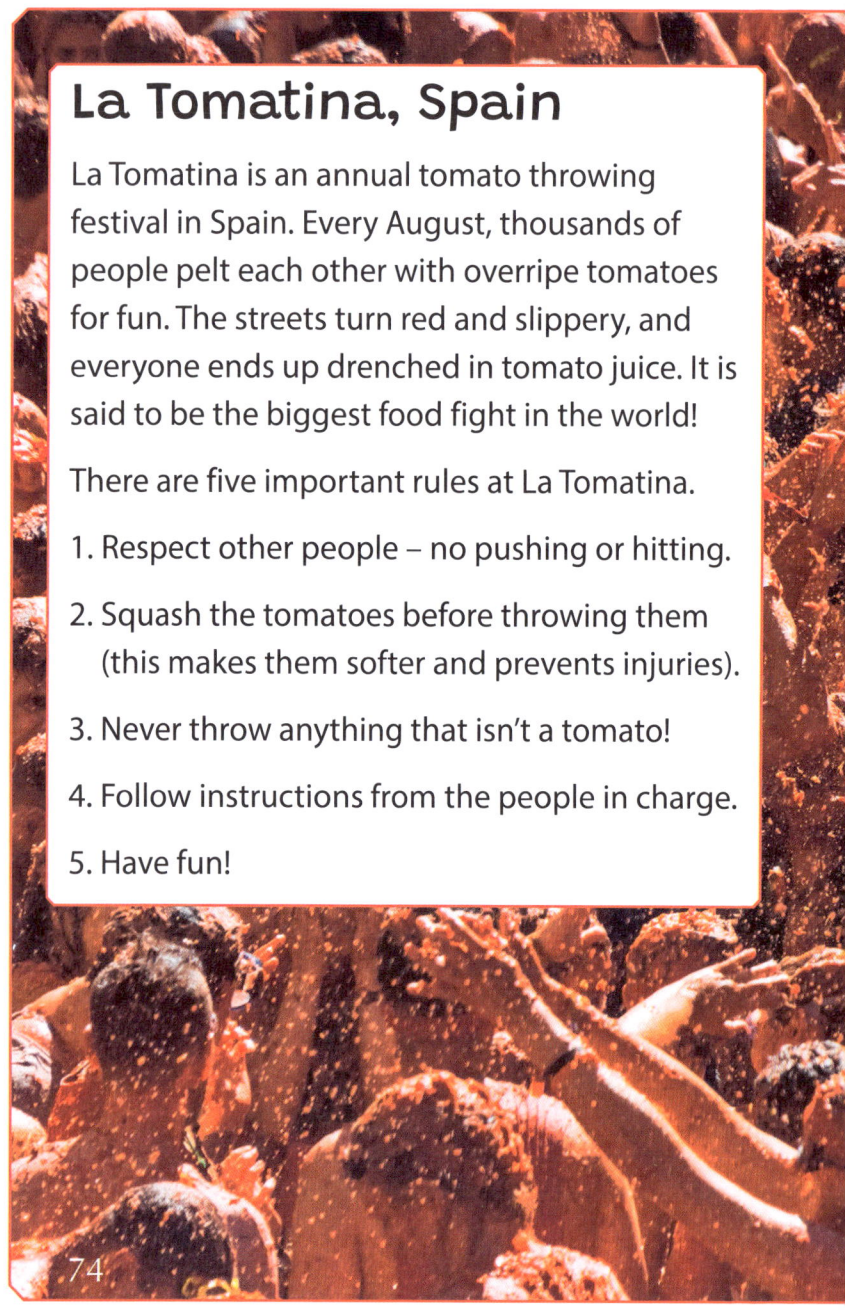

La Tomatina, Spain

La Tomatina is an annual tomato throwing festival in Spain. Every August, thousands of people pelt each other with overripe tomatoes for fun. The streets turn red and slippery, and everyone ends up drenched in tomato juice. It is said to be the biggest food fight in the world!

There are five important rules at La Tomatina.

1. Respect other people – no pushing or hitting.

2. Squash the tomatoes before throwing them (this makes them softer and prevents injuries).

3. Never throw anything that isn't a tomato!

4. Follow instructions from the people in charge.

5. Have fun!

KEY FACTS

People wear old clothes that they don't mind getting stained or ruined, and some people wear goggles because tomato juice can sting.

Tomatoes are grown specially for the festival – these are cheap, overripe and no longer good for eating but perfect for throwing.

Water trucks clean the streets afterwards, as the mess needs a lot of water to clear up.

Tickets are now required to control the crowd, as over 20,000 people attend.

World Gurning Championships, United Kingdom

The gurning competition is one of the highlights of the annual Egremont Crab Fair in Cumbria, United Kingdom. It's an event that is over 700 years old.

Tommy Mattinson has won the gurning competition multiple times.

KEY FACTS

Contestants at the gurning competition have to do some facial gymnastics to pull the most extreme different faces possible to win. You can try one of the popular gurning expressions yourself by pushing your lower jaw as far forward and up as possible and covering your upper lip with your lower lip.

All competitors must wear a horse collar to frame their faces and focus the judges' attention.

There are men's, women's and children's categories, and winners are judged based on creativity, how much they can move their faces and the crowd's reaction. People with faces that can move a lot can be very good at gurning.

Laughter yoga, India

Laughter yoga (*Hasyayoga*) is an exercise programme based on laughter and playfulness, with breathing and meditation. Laughter yoga was first started in Mumbai, India, by Doctor Madan Kataria, who created the first laughter club in a local park in 1995. To keep people laughing when they ran out of jokes, Kataria created laughter exercises.

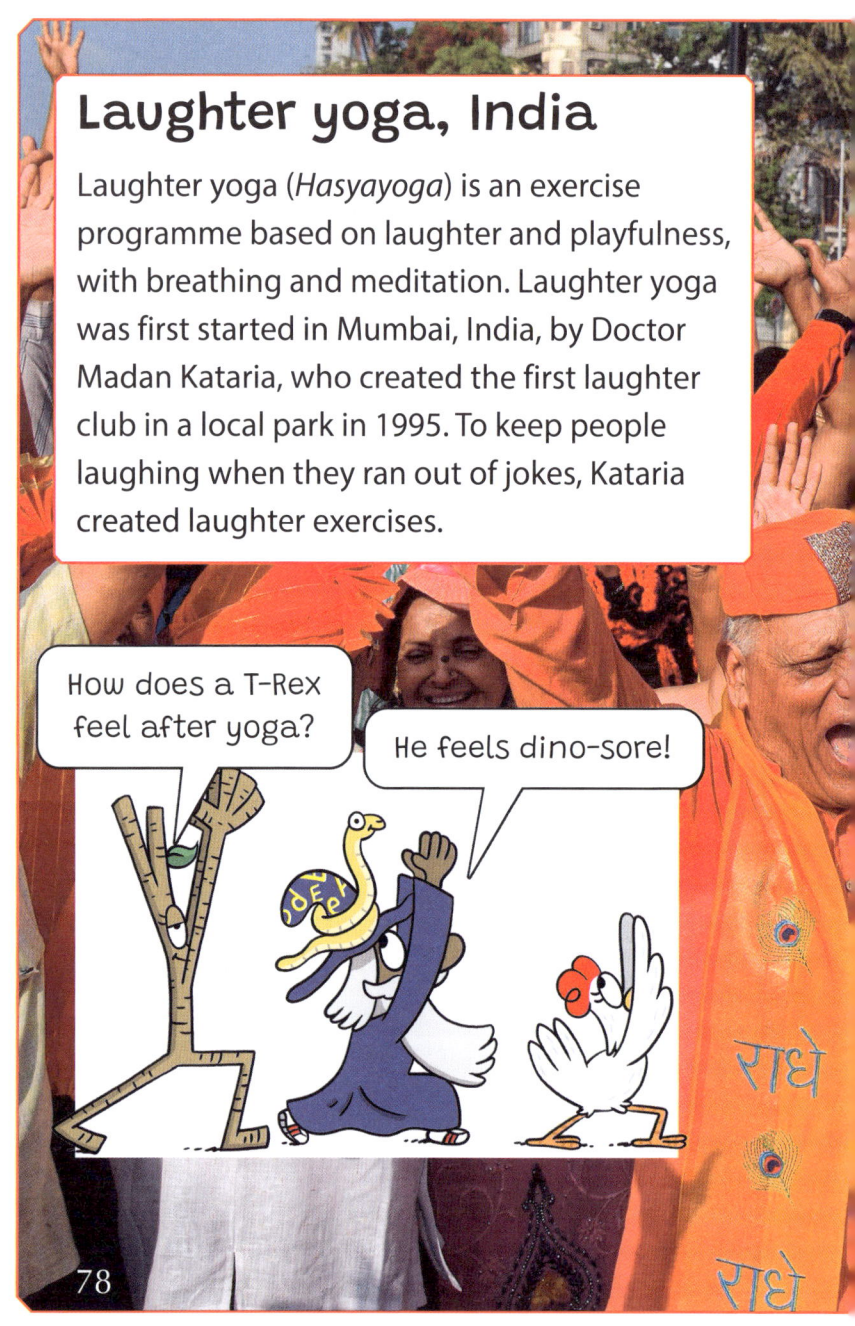

KEY FACTS

The yoga doesn't rely on jokes to make you laugh: instead people just start fake laughing.

It usually starts with clapping, chanting 'Ho ho, ha ha' and exercises to help people relax.

Over time, fake laughter turns into real laughter, especially in group settings.

Monkey Buffet Festival, Thailand

The Monkey Buffet Festival in Thailand is one of the most unusual and fun animal-themed festivals in the world. It takes place in Lopburi, Thailand, to honour local macaque monkeys – thousands of them!

If there were no bananas, what fruit would monkeys choose?

Ape-ricots!

KEY FACTS

A giant banquet of fruits, vegetables and treats is laid out, often stacked in pyramids, towers or creative displays for the monkeys to feast freely.

The monkeys are considered good luck and are associated with Hindu and Buddhist religious traditions.

Monkeys climb onto statues, people and the buffet towers, often stealing from guests and starting food fights. It's chaos!

Locals and tourists take part, often wearing monkey-themed costumes.

Underwater Music Festival, US

In the Florida Keys, in the United States, divers and snorkellers enjoy an underwater concert where music is played through underwater speakers.

This unusual festival happens annually, and has been drawing crowds for over 25 years. People who don't want to dive or snorkel to listen to the music can hear the playlist on the local radio, too.

KEY FACTS

The festival has a serious meaning behind it, though, as **it promotes protection of the marine environment**.

Musicians pretend to play special underwater instruments like a 'trom – bonefish'!

The playlist features ocean-themed tunes, like the song 'Under the Sea' from The Little Mermaid.

People often dress up in ocean-themed costumes, such as mermaids and sea creatures.

World Championship Snail Racing, United Kingdom

The world's only snail racing contest takes place in Congham, England, each year.

KEY FACTS

Snails race on a damp circular 33-centimetre cloth track.

Each snail is marked with a number. They start from the centre of the cloth.

The snails are encouraged with the phrase: Ready, Steady, Slow.

The winning snail gets a silver cup filled with lettuce leaves as a trophy.

The word record for snail racing was set at Congham in 1995. The winning snail, Archie, whizzed round the track in just two minutes!

Competing snails often have names like Zoomer or Racer, but the 2025 winner was called Bilbo Sluggins!

International Hair Freezing Contest, Canada

In February each year, in Takhini Hot Springs, Yukon, Canada, contestants gather to sculpt their frozen hair.

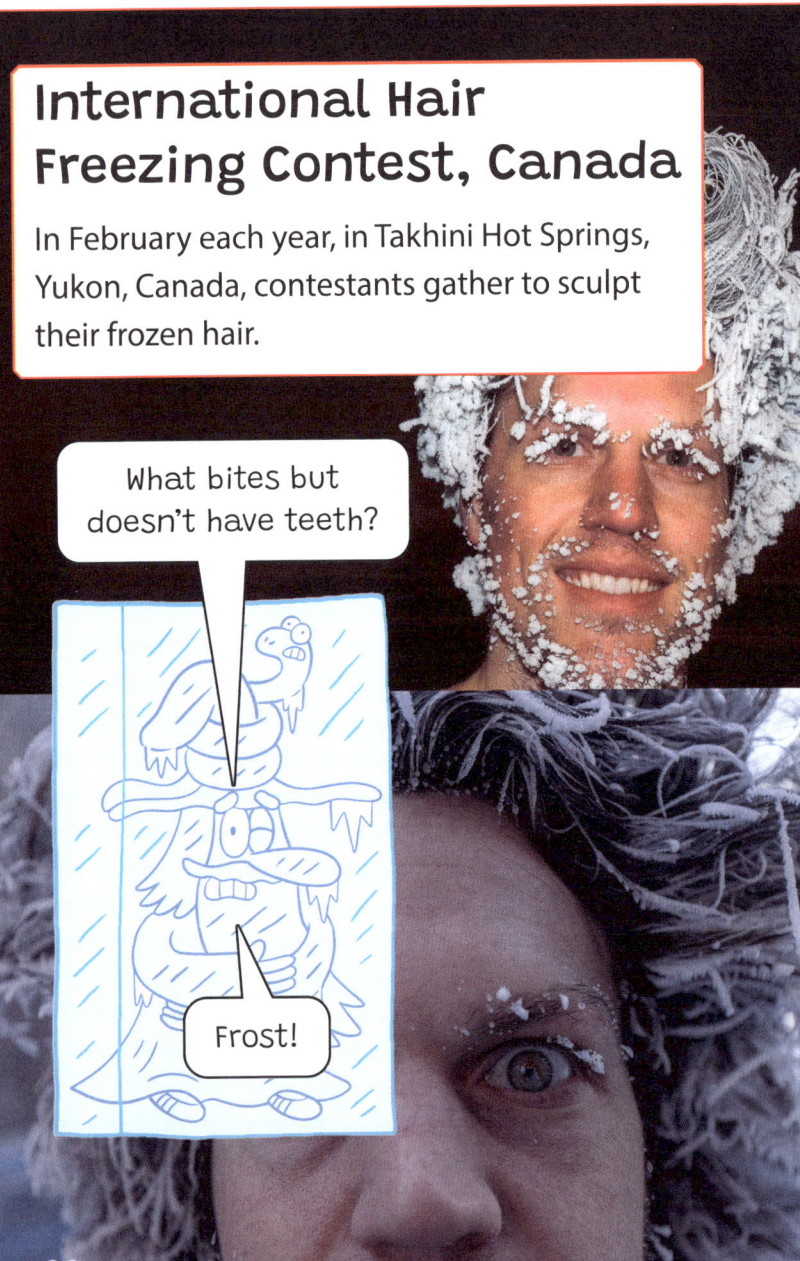

What bites but doesn't have teeth?

Frost!

KEY FACTS

First participants dip their heads in the hot springs (40 degrees Centigrade), completely wetting their hair.

Then, in daily temperatures that can drop to -30 degrees Centigrade, **their hair freezes quickly** as contestants rush to mould it into unique shapes.

Photographers take photos which are used to judge the various categories, including best group and most creative.

BONUS

Festival map

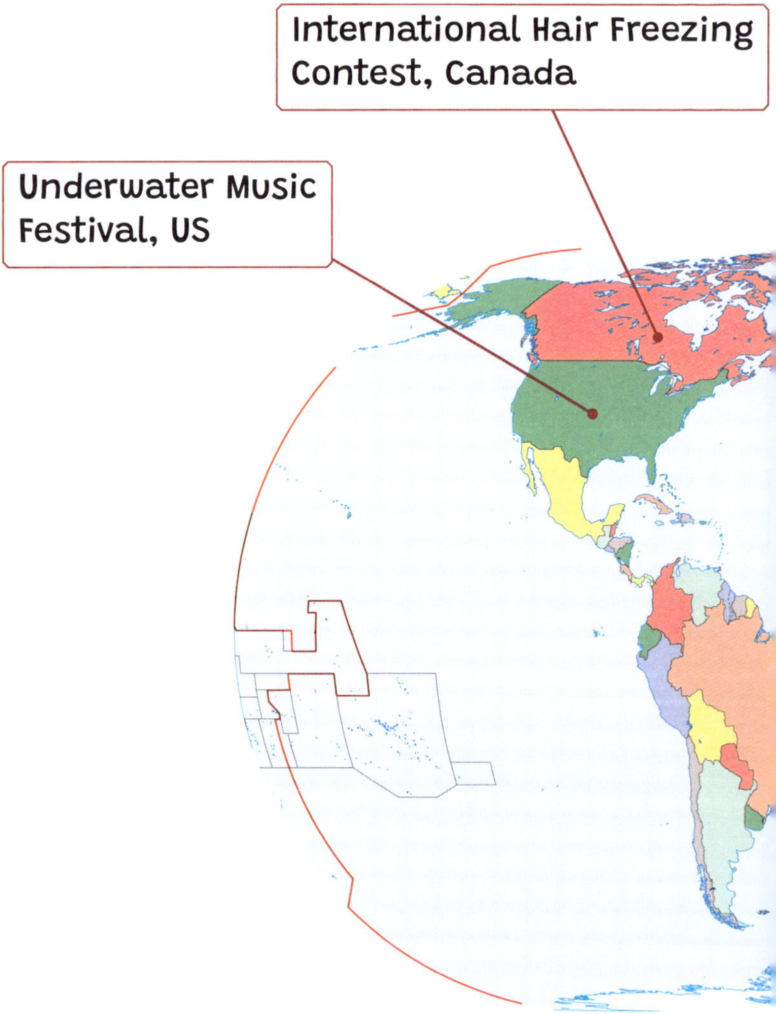

International Hair Freezing Contest, Canada

Underwater Music Festival, US

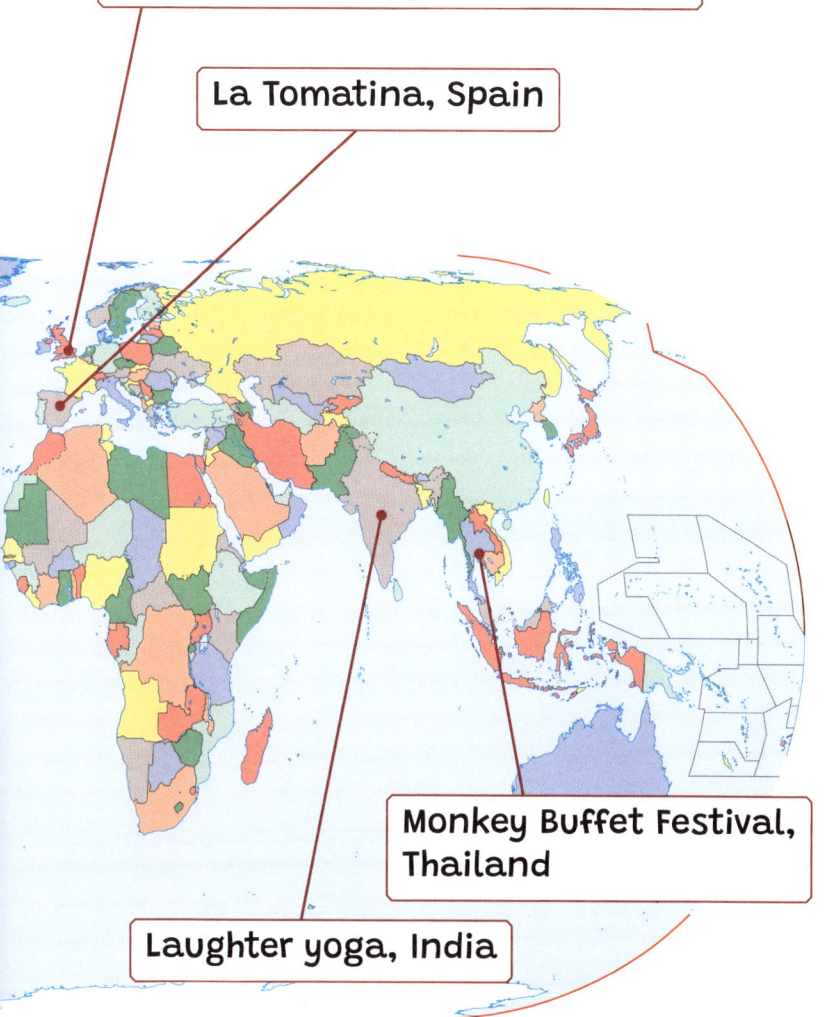

Chapter 6
What happens when we laugh?

Laughter is complex! Did you know that some scientists actually study what happens when we laugh? Gelotology is the term given to the scientific study of laughter, including its effect on our bodies. It explores why we laugh, who we laugh with, how laughing affects our bodies and the important role laughter has in our relationships.

The brain and laughter

Laughing gives our brain a workout! Let's find out what happens in our brains when we hear a joke like this one:

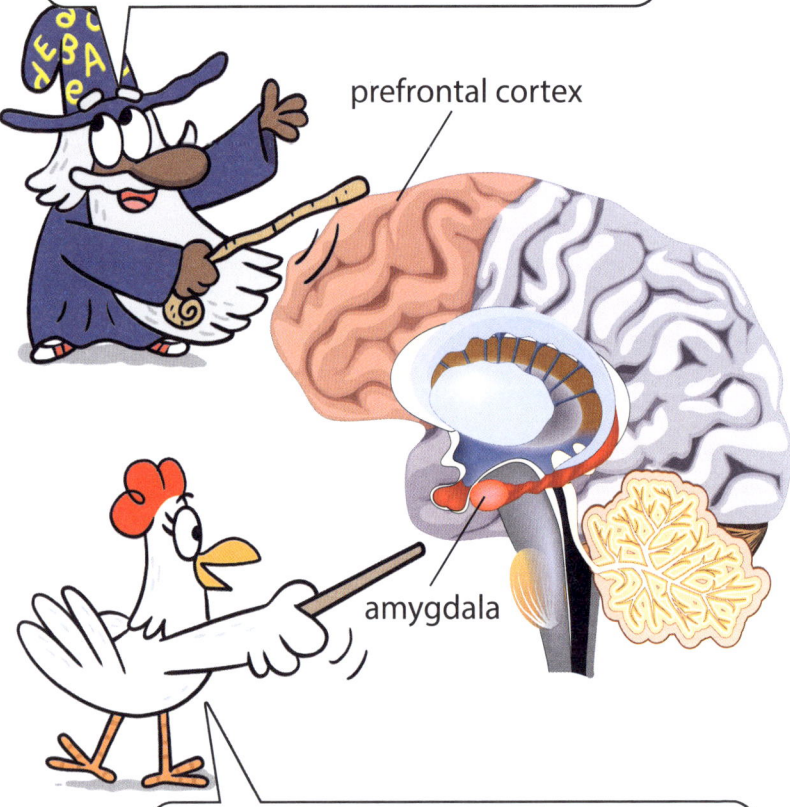

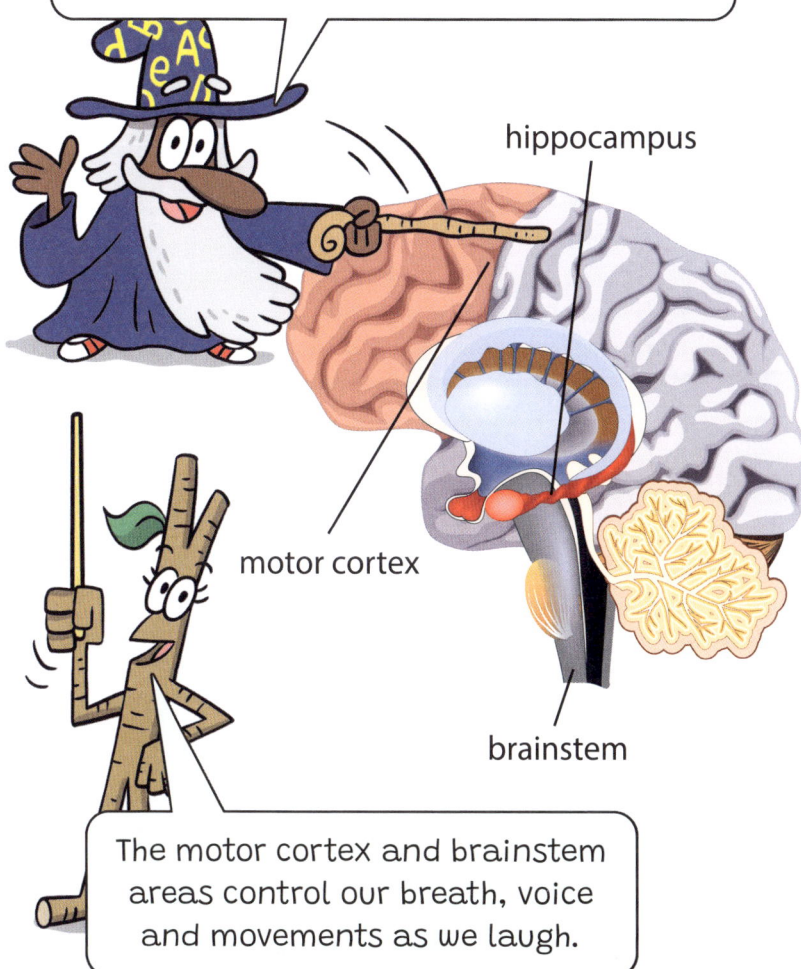

Feel-good chemicals in our bodies

When we laugh, different hormones are released that make us feel good.

Our brains release these chemicals:

dopamine – makes us feel happy

endorphins – natural painkillers

oxytocin – makes us feel close to other people.

Laughter also lowers a chemical in our brains called cortisol, which is a stress hormone. This helps reduce anxiety.

Trying to remember all the names of all these hormones and what they do is stressing me out!

Most people know that watching or reading something funny can help us relax when we are feeling worried or upset. But now scientists are discovering how this works. For example, a study in the United States found that people felt less stressed and had lower cortisol in their brains after watching a funny video.

Is laughing good for us?

Many scientists believe that laughing may have serious health benefits. Some experiments suggest that watching a funny video can help people cope with mild pain. For example, the cold pressor test involved participants immersing their hand into an ice water container for one minute. They did this before and after they had watched a short, funny video. What the scientists discovered was that the participants had a higher ability to tolerate the pain of the icy water AFTER they had watched the video. Patients who watched comedy films also needed less pain medication.

Don't try this at home!

Staying well

It's not just pain that is helped by laughing: enjoying a joke might help to prevent you getting ill. Another experiment showed that people who laughed more were more protected from infections.

Laughing can help your heart rate increase and pump blood around your body – in a similar way to exercise. It can also lower your blood pressure, which is better for your heart. So, laughing can help you stay healthier.

Laughing is an exercise workout for our lungs

Laughter gives our lungs an exercise workout. It involves deeper belly breathing – this is what happens when we laugh out loud. This deeper breathing helps to keep our lungs working well, because it stretches them fully, and this allows them to stay strong.

Have you ever laughed so hard you struggled to breathe? This is because deeper belly laughing can also interfere with our ability to breathe, if we laugh too hard.

Laughing with other people

Laughing at jokes is a way we communicate and bond with other people. Even when we are very young, adults start playing things like the peek-a-boo game with us. This is where they cover their faces then reveal their face with a 'boo' that makes us laugh. We find unexpected things funny even from a young age.

Children laugh many times a day (some people believe 300 to 400 times) whereas adults laugh a lot less – some people think it's fewer than 20 times!

Laughter can help to strengthen relationships within a family or a close group of friends. Lots of families have jokes or funny sayings, which might get repeated countless times over the years! Quite often, these family in-jokes aren't even all that funny to people outside the family. But in a strange way, these repeated jokes and sayings help to build a strong connection between family members.

Laughing together makes friends

Laughter is something we mostly do with other people rather than by ourselves. Studies showed that we are 30 times more likely to laugh in social settings.

Often, the things people laugh about in groups are not actually jokes. They probably wouldn't sound funny if you wrote them down. But by laughing at the same things, people are showing that they like each other and have something in common.

Laughter helps us bond with other people as it helps us trust other people and strengthens our relationships. Groups get stronger through shared laughter as we feel a sense of safety and belonging. Laughter even stops conflicts, as tense situations become more relaxed. So, jokes and laughing can make the world a better place!

Feel-good chemicals

Dopamine

Dopamine is released when we experience something pleasurable. It can encourage us to go after our goals.

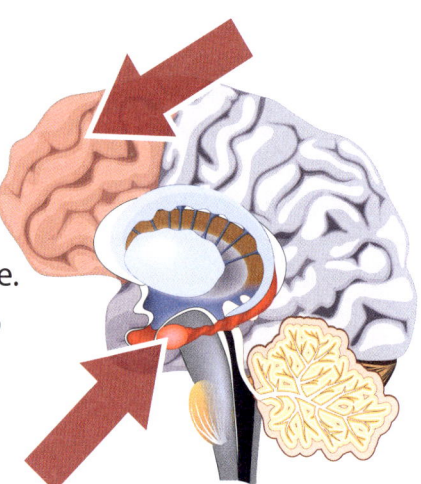

Endorphins

Endorphins are released when we exercise and eat, and they help to reduce our feeling of pain.

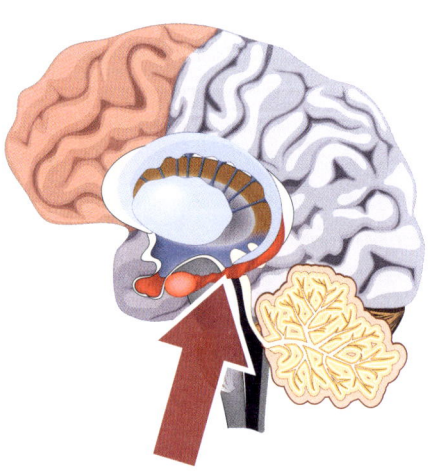

Oxytocin

Oxytocin is released when we are with other people or animals, and when we have hugs. It helps us to feel connected.

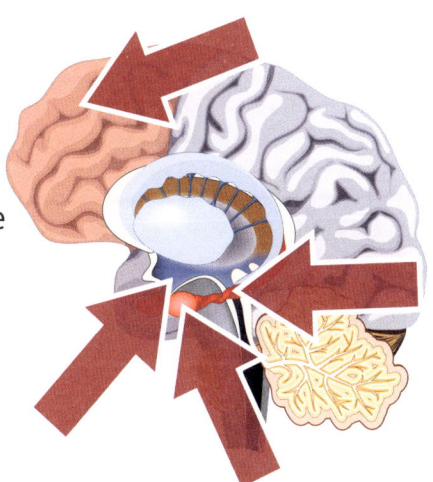

Seratonin

Seratonin helps us to feel happy and also helps with sleep and digestion.

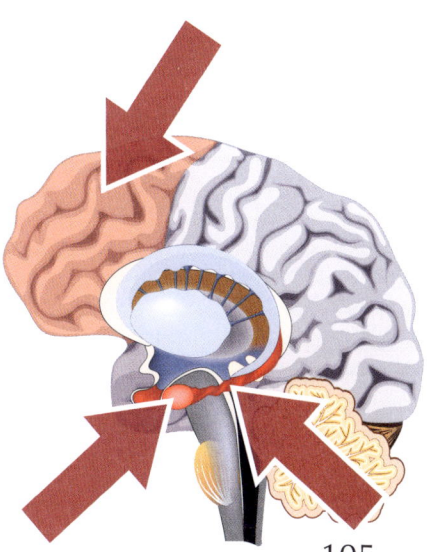

About the author

What do you enjoy most about writing?

Writing is a lot of fun – from researching fascinating topics, to creating interesting characters and using my imagination. I also enjoy seeing my characters come to life through the illustrations. It was absolutely brilliant to meet all the characters for the first time – they made me laugh.

Ayesha Braganza

What was the most interesting thing you learnt when researching and writing this book?

I loved discovering that humans have laughed about some of the same things for thousands of years – like Roman fart cushions!

Why did you want to write a book about humour?

Learning about jokes is really interesting. I have laughed a lot, but I've also discovered intriguing facts about our bodies, brains, other people and society. I'm not sure I realised what a serious business humour actually is – it's amazing that it can actually influence our physical health and help us not get ill.

Do you have a favourite joke or type of humour?
Being a writer, I love words and playing with them. Wordplay just feels WRITE!

How did you come up with the idea for this book?
I wondered about the first chicken joke, and in researching this book I found out more about this kind of joke. Can you remember when chicken jokes first became popular?

What was the last thing that made you laugh out loud?
My niece and nephew, Zoe and Alex, told me a joke recently, but it's a bit rude …
What is a lady called who has two toilets on her head?
LuLu!

What do you hope readers will get from the book?
I hope they will laugh a lot and share some of these jokes with their friends and families. I also hope they will learn why laughter is important. Maybe they will think about what kinds of humour make them laugh most – slapstick or wordplay, or maybe a type of humour I haven't even thought about!

Do you think humour will continue to change?
Yes, this book has showed how humour has changed. However, it also shows that jokes – especially wordless ones – unite us as human beings not only from different parts of the world, but over thousands of years.

About the illustrator

Did you always want to be an illustrator?
Yes. I always wanted to draw. I knew I wanted to be an illustrator from a very young age.

How did you get into illustrating?
I've always published comics and graphic humour in Argentina. Then I went to the Bologna Book Fair in 2011 and met the Advocate Art agency. Thanks to them, I began illustrating books for book publishers around the world.

Emiliano Migliardo

Do you use pens and paints or do you work digitally?
I usually make a first sketch on paper with a blue pencil, then I redraw it with more detail in black pancil. Then I scan the sketch and work on it digitally.

Do you always draw cartoons, or sometimes serious illustrations?
I specialise in humorous drawings, funny illustrations, comics, and caricatures. Sometimes when I illustrate school textbooks, it can be a little more serious, but I always try to give them a touch of fun when I can.

Which character was the most fun to draw?
I think they're all fun. Each one has something special.

What was your favourite cartoon in the book to illustrate?
I really enjoyed illustrating the character of the slapstick.

Did anything surprise you about the history of jokes?
There are so many interesting facts I didn't know; it's a great book.

Did you know any of the people in the book from films or TV?
Yes … I'm a big fan of comedy!

What's your favourite joke?
It would be impossible to choose my favorite joke, but I remember an episode of The Three Stooges called 'Dizzy doctors'.

The Stooges get a job selling 'Brighto' and they offer this product to people on the street: 'Brighto! Brighto! Brighto!' they shout, when suddenly, Curly stops and asks Moe: 'Hey Moe, what's this stuff for anyway?' Moe hits him and answers: 'It's for selling!'

Do you have any favourite programmes that make you laugh?
So many, these are some of my favourites: Benny Hill, Monty Python, The Three Stooges, Peanuts, Don Martin, Jerry Seinfeld, Ricky Gervais, The Simpsons, Mel Brooks and Seth MacFarlane.

Book chat

Have you ever read a book like this before?

What was the most interesting thing you learnt from this book?

Do you have a favourite joke?

What type of humour do you find funny?

If you could make up a different title for this book, what would it be?

Was there anything that surprised you in this book?

Who would you recommend this book to and why?

Book challenge:

Draw your own fun character and write a joke for them to tell.

Collins BIG CAT

Published by Collins
An imprint of HarperCollins*Publishers*

The News Building
1 London Bridge Street
London
SE1 9GF
UK

Macken House
39/40 Mayor Street Upper
Dublin 1
D01 C9W8
Ireland

© HarperCollins*Publishers* Limited 2025

Maps © Collins Bartholomew 2025

10 9 8 7 6 5 4 3 2 1

ISBN 978-0-00-876793-8

All rights reserved. No part of this publication may be reproduced, stored in a retrieval system, or transmitted in any form by any means, electronic, mechanical, photocopying, recording or otherwise, without the prior written permission of the Publisher or a licence permitting restricted copying in the United Kingdom issued by the Copyright Licensing Agency Ltd, 5th Floor, Shackleton House, 4 Battle Bridge Lane, London SE1 2HX.

Without limiting the exclusive rights of any author, contributor or the publisher of this publication, any unauthorised use of this publication to train generative artificial intelligence (AI) technologies is expressly prohibited. HarperCollins also exercise their rights under Article 4(3) of the Digital Single Market Directive 2019/790 and expressly reserve this publication from the text and data mining exception.

British Library Cataloguing-in-Publication Data
A catalogue record for this publication is available from the British Library.

Download the teaching notes and word cards to accompany this book at:
http://littlewandle.org.uk/signupfluency/

Get the latest Collins Big Cat news at
collins.co.uk/collinsbigcat

Author: Ayesha Braganza
Illustrator: Emiliano Migliardo (Advocate Art)
Publisher: Laura White
Commissioning editor and
       product manager: Caroline Green
Series editor: Charlotte Raby
Development editor: Catherine Baker
Project manager: Emily Hooton
Copyeditor: Sally Byford
Proofreader: Catherine Dakin
Cover designer: Sarah Finan
Typesetter: 2Hoots Publishing Services Ltd
Production controller: Katharine Willard

Printed in the UK.

MIX
Paper | Supporting
responsible forestry
FSC™ C007454

This book contains FSC™ certified paper and other controlled sources to ensure responsible forest management.

For more information visit: www.harpercollins.co.uk/green

Made with responsibly sourced paper and vegetable ink

Scan to see how we are reducing our environmental impact.

Acknowledgements
The publishers gratefully acknowledge the permission granted to reproduce the copyright material in this book. Every effort has been made to trace copyright holders and to obtain their permission for the use of copyright material. The publishers will gladly receive any information enabling them to rectify any error or omission at the first opportunity.

p8 fast-stock/Shutterstock, p13 Beautifulimages1717/Shutterstock, p23 & 36tr The Picture Art Collection/Alamy, p30 & 37bl Allstar Picture Library Ltd/Alamy, p31 & 36br CBS Photo Archive/Getty images, p32 Allstar Picture Library Ltd/Alamy, p33 & 36bl Wikimedia Commons, p35 Koyu/Shutterstock, p36tl Didit hutomo/Shutterstock, p41 The History Collection/Alamy, p50 Jesus Pelayo Diaz/Shutterstock, p57 Rawpixel.com/Shutterstock, p59 GRANGER - Historical Picture Archive/Alamy, p60 Chronicle/Alamy, p63 Sueddeutsche Zeitung Photo/Alamy, p65 Everett Collection Inc/Alamy, p66 Pictorial Press Ltd/Alamy, pp74–75 Keren Su/China Span/Alamy, p76 John Li/Stringer/Getty Images, pp78–79 ZUMA Press, Inc./Alamy, pp80–81 ZUMA Press, Inc./Alamy, pp84–85 Action Plus Sports Images/Alamy, p86t Scalia Media/Shutterstock, p86b Scalia Media/Getty Images, p87t Scalia Media/Shutterstock, p87b Scalia Media/Getty Images, pp92, 93, 104, 105 Designua/Shutterstock, p96 PamelaJoeMcFarlane/Getty Images, p100 Jacob Lund/Shutterstock, p102 Inside Creative House/Shutterstock.